Suppressed Desires

By George Cram Cook
and Susan Glaspell

NEW YORK

1917

BROADWAY PLAY PUBLISHING INC
New York
www.broadwayplaypub.com
info@broadwayplaypub.com

Suppressed Desires

A Freudian Comedy in Two Scenes

By GEORGE CRAM COOK

and

SUSAN GLASPELL

As Produced by the Provincetown Players, New York City

HENRIETTA BREWSTER	SUSAN GLASPELL
STEPHEN BREWSTER	GEORGE CRAM COOK
MABEL	MARY PYNE

PLACE—*A New York Apartment*
TIME—*Today*

A period of two weeks is supposed to elapse between the first and second scenes.

COPYRIGHT 1916 — SUSAN GLASPELL

Application for permission to perform this play must be made to the Provincetown Players, 139 Macdougal Street, New York; no performance can take place without their permission.

Suppressed Desires

Scene I

The stage represents a studio, used as living and dining room in an upper story, Washington Square South. Through an immense north window in the back wall appear tree tops and the upper part of the Washington Arch. Beyond it you look up Fifth Avenue. There are rugs, bookcases, a divan. Near the window is a big table, loaded at one end with serious-looking books and austere scientific periodicals. At the other end are architect's drawings, blue prints, dividing compasses, square, ruler, etc. There is a door in each side wall. Near the one to the spectator's right stands a costumer with hats and coats, masculine and feminine. There is a breakfast table set for three, but only two seated at it—namely Henrietta and Stephen Brewster. As the curtains withdraw Steve pushes back his coffee cup and sits dejected.

HENRIETTA: It isn't the coffee. Steve dear. There's nothing the matter with the coffee. There's something the matter with *you*.

STEVE: (*Doggedly.*) There may be something the matter with my stomach.

HENRIETTA: (*Scornfully.*) Your stomach! The trouble is not with your stomach but in your sub-conscious mind.

STEVE: Subconscious piffle! (*Takes morning paper and tries to read.*)

HENRIETTA: Steve, you never used to be so disagreeable. You certainly have got some sort of a complex. You're all inhibited. You're no longer open to new ideas. You won't listen to a word about psychoanalysis.

STEVE: A word! I've listened to volumes!

HENRIETTA: You've ceased to be creative in architecture—your work isn't going well. You're not sleeping well——

STEVE: How can I sleep, Henrietta, when you're always waking me up in the night to find out what I'm dreaming?

HENRIETTA: But dreams are so important, Steve. If you'd tell yours to Dr. Russell he'd find out exacty what's wrong with you.

STEVE: There's nothing wrong with me.

HENRIETTA: You don't even talk as well as you used to.

STEVE: Talk? I can't say a thing without you looking at me in that dark fashion you have when you're on the trail of a complex.

HENRIETTA: This very irritability indicates that you're suffering from some suppressed desire.

STEVE: I'm suffering from a suppressed desire for a little peace.

HENRIETTA: Dr. Russell is doing simply wonderful things with nervous cases. Won't you go to him, Steve?

STEVE (*Slamming down his newspaper*): No, Henrietta, I won't!

HENRIETTA: But, Stephen—!

STEVE: Tst! I hear Mabel coming. Let's not be at each other's throats the first day of her visit. (*He takes out cigarettes. Enter Mabel from door left, the side opposite Steve, so that he is facing her. She is wearing a rather fussy negligee and breakfast cap in contrast to Henrietta, who wears "radical" clothes. Mabel is what is called plump.*)

MABEL: Good morning.

HENRIETTA: Oh, here you are, little sister.

STEVE: Good morning, Mabel. (*Mabel nods to him and turns, her face lighting up, to Henrietta.*)

HENRIETTA: (*Giving Mabel a hug as she leans against her.*) It's so good to have you here. I was going to let you sleep, thinking you'd be tired after the long trip. Sit down. There'll be fresh toast in a minute and (*rising from her chair*) will you have——

MABEL: Oh; I ought to have told you, Henrietta. Don't get anything for me. I'm not eating any breakfast.

HENRIETTA: (*At first in mere surprise.*) Not eating breakfast? (*She sits down, then leans toward Mabel and scrutinizes her.*)

STEVE: (*Half to himself.*) The psychoanalytical look!

HENRIETTA: Mabel, why are you not eating breakfast?

MABEL: (*A little startled.*) Why, no particular reason. I just don't care much for breakfast, and they say it keeps down—that is, it's a good thing to go without it.

HENRIETTA: Don't you sleep well? Did you sleep well last night?

MABEL: Oh, yes, I slept all right. Yes, I slept fine last night, only (*laughing*) I did have the funniest dream!

STEVE: S—h! S—t!

HENRIETTA: (*Moving closer.*) And what did you dream, Mabel?

STEVE: Look-a-here, Mabel, I feel it's my duty to put you on. Don't tell Henrietta your dreams. If you do she'll find out that you have an underground desire to kill your father and marry your mother——

HENRIETTA: Don't be absurd, Stephen Brewster. (*Sweetly to Mabel.*) What was your dream, dear?

MABEL: (*Laughing.*) Well, I dreamed I was a hen.

HENRIETTA: A hen?

MABEL: Yes; and I was pushing along through a crowd as fast as I could, but being a hen I couldn't walk very fast—it was like having a tight skirt, you know;

and there was some sort of creature in a blue cap—you know how mixed up dreams are—and it kept shouting after me and saying, "Step, Hen! Step, Hen!" until I got all excited and just couldn't move at all.

HENRIETTA: (*Resting chin in palm and peering.*) You say you became much excited?

MABEL: (*Laughing.*) Oh, yes; I was in a terrible state.

HENRIETTA: (*Leaning back, murmurs.*) This is significant.

STEVE: She dreams she's a hen. She is told to step lively. She becomes violently agitated. What can it mean?

HENRIETTA: (*Turning impatiently from him.*) Mabel, do you know anything about psychoanalysis?

MABEL: (*Feebly.*) Oh—not much. No—I—(*brightening.*) It's something about the war, isn't it?

STEVE: Not that kind of war.

MABEL: (*Abashed.*) I thought it might be the name of a new explosive.

STEVE: It *is*.

MABEL: (*Apologetically to Henrietta, who is frowning.*) You see, Henrietta, I—we do not live in touch with intellectual things, as you do. Bob being a dentist—somehow—our friends——

STEVE: (*Softly.*) Oh, to be a dentist! (*Goes to window and stands looking out.*)

HENRIETTA: Don't you ever see anything more of that editorial writer—what was his name?

MABEL: Lyman Eggleston?

HENRIETTA: Yes, Eggleston. He was in touch with things. Don't you see him?

MABEL: Yes, I see him once in a while. Bob doesn't like him very well.

HENRIETTA: Your husband does not like Lyman Eggleston? (*Mysteriously.*) Mabel, are you perfectly happy with your husband?

STEVE: (*Sharply.*) Oh, come now, Henrietta—that's going a little strong!

HENRIETTA: Are you perfectly happy with him, Mabel? (*Steve goes to work-table.*)

MABEL: Why—yes—I guess so. Why—of course I am!

HENRIETTA: Are you happy? Or do you only think you are? Or do you only think you *ought* to be?

MABEL: Why, Henrietta, I don't know what you mean!

STEVE: (*Seizes stack of books and magazines and dumps them on the breakfast table.*) This is what she means, Mabel. Psychoanalysis. My work-table groans with it. Books by Freud, the new Messiah; books by Jung, the new St. Paul; the Psycho-analytical Review back numbers two-fifty per.

MABEL: But what's it all about?

STEVE: All about your sub-un-non-conscious mind and desires you know not of. They may be doing you a great deal of harm. You may go crazy with them. Oh, yes! People are doing it right and left. Your dreaming you're a hen—— (*Shakes his head darkly.*)

HENRIETTA: Any fool can ridicule anything.

MABEL: (*Hastily, to avert a quarrel.*) But what do you say it is, Henrietta?

STEVE: (*Looking at his watch.*) Oh, if Henrietta's going to start that! (*He goes to his work-table, and during Henrietta's next speech settles himself and sharpens a lead pencil.*)

HENRIETTA: It's like this, Mabel. You want something. You think you can't have it. You think it's wrong. So you try to think you don't want it. Your mind protects you—avoids pain—by refusing to think the forbidden thing. But it's there just the same. It stays there shut up in your unconscious mind, and it festers.

STEVE: Sort of an ingrowing mental toenail.

HENRIETTA: Precisely. The forbidden impulse is there full of energy which has simply got to do something. It breaks into your consciousness in disguise, masks itself in dreams, makes all sorts of trouble. In extreme cases it drives you insane.

MABEL: (*With a gesture of horror.*) Oh!

HENRIETTA: (*Reassuring.*) But psychoanalysis has found out how to save us from that. It brings into consciousness the suppressed desire that was making all the trouble. Psychoanalysis is simply the latest scientific method of preventing and curing insanity.

STEVE: (*From his table.*) It is also the latest scientific method of separating families.

HENRIETTA: (*Mildly.*) Families that ought to be separated.

STEVE: The Dwights, for instance. You must have met them, Mabel, when you were here before. Helen was living, apparently, in peace and happiness with good old Joe. Well—she went to this psychoanalyzer—she was "psyched," and biff!—bang!—home she comes with an unsuppressed desire to leave her husband. (*He starts work, drawing lines on a drawing board with a T-square.*)

MABEL: How terrible! Yes, I remember Helen Dwight. But—but did she have such a desire?

STEVE: First she'd known of it.

MABEL: And she *left* him?

HENRIETTA: (*Coolly.*) Yes, she did.

MABEL: Wasn't he good to her?

HENRIETTA: Why yes, good enough.

MABEL: Wasn't he kind to her?

HENRIETTA: Oh, yes—kind to her.

MABEL: And she left her good kind husband—!

HENRIETTA: Oh, Mabel! 'Left her good, kind husband!' How naive—forgive me, dear, but how bourgeoise you are! She came to know herself. And she had the courage!

MABEL: I may be very naive and—bourgeoise—but I don't see the good of a new science that breaks up homes. (*Steve claps hands, applauding.*)

STEVE: In enlightening Mabel, we mustn't neglect to mention the case of Art Holden's private secretary, Mary Snow, who has just been informed of her suppressed desire for her employer.

MABEL: Why, I think it is terrible, Henrietta! It would be better if we didn't know such things about ourselves.

HENRIETTA: No, Mabel, that is the old way.

MABEL: But—but her employer? Is he married?

STEVE: (*Grunts.*) Wife and four children.

MABEL: Well, then, what good does it do the girl to be told she has a desire for him? There's nothing that can be done about it.

HENRIETTA: Old institutions will have to be reshaped so that something can be done in such cases. It happens, Mabel, that this suppressed desire was on the point of landing Mary Snow in the insane asylum. Are you so tight-minded that you'd rather have her in the insane asylum than break the conventions?

MABEL: But—but have people always had these awful suppressed desires?

HENRIETTA: Always.

STEVE: But they've just been discovered.

HENRIETTA: The harm they do has just been discovered. And free, sane people must face the fact that they have to be dealt with.

MABEL: (*Stoutly.*) I don't believe they have them in Chicago.

HENRIETTA: (*Business of giving Mabel up.*) People "have them" wherever the living Libido—the center of the soul's energy—is in conflict with petrified moral codes. That means everywhere in civilization. Psychoanalysis——

STEVE: Good God! I've got the roof in the cellar!

HENRIETTA: The roof in the cellar!

STEVE: (*Holding plan at arm's length.*) That's what psychoanalysis does!

HENRIETTA: That's what psychoanalysis could *un*-do. Is it any wonder I'm concerned about Steve? He dreamed the other night that the walls of his room melted away and he found himself alone in a forest. Don't you see how significant it is for an architect to have *walls* slip away from him? It symbolizes his loss of grip in his work. There's some suppressed desire——

STEVE: (*Hurling his ruined plan viciously to the floor.*) Suppressed hell!

HENRIETTA: You speak more truly than you know. It is through suppressions that hells are formed in us.

MABEL: (*Looking at Steve, who is tearing his hair.*) Don't you think it would be a good thing, Henrietta, if we went somewhere else? (*They rise and begin to pick up the dishes. Mabel drops a plate which breaks. Henrietta draws up short and looks at her—the psychoanalytic look.*) I'm sorry, Henrietta. One of the Spode plates, too. (*Surprised and resentful as Henrietta continues to peer at her.*) Don't take it so to heart, Henrietta.

HENRIETTA: I can't help taking it to heart.

MABEL: I'll get you another. (*Pause. More sharply as Henrietta does not answer.*) I said I'll get you another plate, Henrietta.

HENRIETTA: It's not the plate.

MABEL: For heaven's sake, what is it then?

HENRIETTA: It's the significant little false movement that made you drop it.

MABEL: Well, I suppose everyone makes a false movement once in a while.

HENRIETTA: Yes, Mabel, but these false movements all mean something.

MABEL: (*About to cry.*) I don't think that's very nice! It was just because I happened to think of that Mabel Snow you were talking about——

HENRIETTA: *Mabel* Snow!

MABEL: Snow—Snow—well, what was her name, then?

HENRIETTA: Her name is Mary. You substituted *your own* name for hers.

MABEL: Well, *Mary* Snow, then; *Mary* Snow. I never heard her name but once. I don't see anything to make such a fuss about.

HENRIETTA: (*Gently.*) Mabel dear—mistakes like that in names——

MABEL: (*Desperately.*) They don't mean something, too, do they?

HENRIETTA: (*Gently.*) I am sorry, dear, but they do.

MABEL: But I am always doing that!

HENRIETTA: (*After a start of horror.*) My poor little sister, tell me all about it.

MABEL: About what?

HENRIETTA: About your not being happy. About your longing for another sort of life.

MABEL: But I *don't*.

HENRIETTA: Ah, I understand these things, dear. You feel Bob is limiting you to a life which you do not feel free——

MABEL: Henrietta! When did I ever say such a thing?

HENRIETTA: You said you are not in touch with things intellectual. You showed your feeling that it is Bob's profession—that has engendered a resentment which has colored your whole life with him.

MABEL: Why—Henrietta!

HENRIETTA: Don't be afraid of me, little sister. There's nothing can shock me or turn me from you. I am not like that. I wanted you to come for this visit because I had a feeling that you needed more from life than you were getting. No one of these things I have seen would excite my suspicion. It's the combination. You don't eat breakfast; you make false moves; you substitute your own name for the name of another *whose love is misdirected*. You're nervous; you look queer; in your eyes there's a frightened look that is most unlike you. And this dream. A *hen*—come with me this afternoon to Dr. Russell! Your whole life may be at stake, Mabel.

MABEL: (*Gasping.*) Henrietta, I—you—you always were the smartest in the family, and all that, but—this is terrible! I don't think we *ought* to think such things, and (*brightening.*) Why, I'll tell you why I dreamed I was a hen. It was because last night, telling about that time in Chicago, you said I was as mad as a wet hen.

HENRIETTA: (*Superior.*) Did you dream you were a *wet* hen?

MABEL: (*Forced to admit it.*) No.

HENRIETTA: No. You dreamed you were a *dry* hen. And why, being a hen, were you urged to step?

MABEL: Maybe it's because when I am getting on a street car it always irritates me to have them call "Step lively."

HENRIETTA: No, Mabel, that is only a child's view of it—if you will forgive me. You see merely the elements used in the dream. You do not see into the dream; you do not see its meaning. This dream of the hen——

STEVE: Hen—hen—wet hen—dry hen—mad hen! (*Jumps up in a rage.*) Let me out of this!

HENRIETTA: (*Hastily picking up dishes, speaks soothingly.*) Just a minute, dear, and we'll have things so you can work in quiet. Mabel and I are going to sit in my room. (*She goes out with both hands full of dishes.*)

STEVE: (*Seizing hat and coat from the costumer.*) I'm going to be psychoanalyzed. I'm going now! I'm going straight to that infallible doctor of hers—that priest of this new religion. If he's got honesty enough to tell Henrietta there's nothing the matter with my unconscious mind, perhaps I can be let alone about it, and then I *will* be all right. (*From the door in a low voice.*) Don't tell Henrietta I'm going. It might take weeks, and I couldn't stand all the talk. (*Exit desperately.*)

Enter Henrietta.

HENRIETTA: Where's Steve? Gone? (*With hopeless gesture.*) You see how impatient he is—how unlike himself! I tell you, Mabel, I am nearly distracted about Steve.

MABEL: I think he's' a little distracted, too.

HENRIETTA: Well, if he's gone—you might as well stay here. I have a committee meeting at the book-shop, and will have to leave you to yourself for an hour or two. (*As she puts her hat on, her eye, lighting up almost carnivorously, falls on an enormous volume on the floor beside the work-table. The book has been half hidden from the audience by the wastebasket. She picks it up and carries it around the table toward Mabel.*) Here, dear, is one of the simplest statements of psycho-analysis. You just read this and then we can talk more intelligently. (*Mabel takes volume and staggers back under its weight to chair rear center, Henrietta goes to outer door, stops and asks abruptly.*) How old is Lyman Eggleston?

MABEL: (*Promptly.*) He isn't forty yet. Why, what made you ask that, Henrietta? (*As she turns her head to look at Henrietta her hands move toward the upper corners of the book balanced on her knees.*)

HENRIETTA: Oh, nothing. Au revoir. (*Exit.*)

(*Mabel stares at the ceiling. The book slides to the floor. She starts; looks at the book, then at the broken plate on the table.*) The plate! The book! (*She lifts her eyes, leans forward, elbow on knee, chin on knuckles and plaintively queries.*) Am I happy?

CURTAIN.

SECOND ACT.

SCENE II

The stage is set as in Scene I, except that the breakfast table has been removed or set back against the wall. During the first few minutes the dusk of a winter afternoon deepens. Out of the darkness spring rows of double street-lights almost meeting in the distance. Henrietta is disclosed at the psychoanalytical end of Steve's worktable. Surrounded by open books and periodicals she is writing. Steve enters briskly.

STEVE: What are you doing, my dear?

HENRIETTA: My paper for the Liberal Club.

STEVE: Your paper on——?

HENRIETTA: On a subject which does not have your sympathy.

STEVE: Oh, I'm not sure I'm wholly out of sympathy with psychoanalysis, Henrietta. You worked it so hard. I couldn't even take a bath without it's meaning something.

HENRIETTA: (Loftily.) I talked it because I knew you needed it.

STEVE: You haven't said much about it these last two weeks. Uh—your faith in it hasn't weakened any?

HENRIETTA: Weakened? It's grown stronger with each new thing I've come to know. And Mabel. She is with Dr. Russell now. Dr. Russell is wonderful. From what Mabel tells me I believe his analysis is going to prove that I was right. Today I discovered a remarkable confirmation of my theory in the hen-dream.

STEVE: What is your theory?

HENRIETTA: Well, you know about Lyman Eggleston. I've wondered about him. I've never seen him, but I know he's less bourgeois than Mabel's other friends—more intellectual—and (*significantly*) she doesn't see much of him because Bob doesn't like him.

STEVE: But what's the confirmation?

HENRIETTA: Today I noticed the first syllable of his name.

STEVE: Ly?

HENRIETTA: No—egg.

STEVE: Egg?

HENRIETTA: (*Patiently.*) Mabel dreamed she was a *hen*. (*Steve laughs.*) You wouldn't laugh if you knew how important names are in interpreting dreams. Freud is full of just such cases in which a whole hidden complex is revealed by a single significant syllable—like this egg.

STEVE: Doesn't the traditional relation of hen and egg suggest rather a maternal feeling?

HENRIETTA: There is something maternal in Mabel's love, of course, but that's only one element.

STEVE: Well, suppose Mabel hasn't a suppressed desire to be this gentleman's mother, but his beloved. What's to be done about it? What about Bob? Don't you think it's going to be a little rough on him?

HENRIETTA: That can't be helped. Bob, like everyone else must face the facts of life. If Dr. Russell should arrive independently at this same interpretation I shall not hesitate to advise Mabel to leave her present husband.

STEVE: Um—uh! (*The lights go up on Fifth Avenue. Steve goes to the window and looks out.*) How long is it we've lived here, Henrietta?

HENRIETTA: Why, this is the third year, Steve.

STEVE: I—we—one would miss this view if one went away, wouldn't one?

HENRIETTA: How strangely you speak! Oh, Stephen, I *wish* you'd go to Dr. Russell. Don't think my fears have abated because I've been able to restrain myself. I had to on account of Mabel. But now, dear—won't you go?

STEVE: I—(*He breaks off, turns on the light, then comes and sits beside Henrietta.*) How long have we been married, Henrietta?

HENRIETTA: Stephen, I don't understand you! You must go to Dr. Russell.

STEVE: I *have* gone.

HENRIETTA: You—what?

STEVE: (*Jauntily.*) Yes, Henrietta, I've been psyched.

HENRIETTA: You went to Dr. Russell?

STEVE: The same.

HENRIETTA: And what did he say?

STEVE: He said—I—I was a little surprised by what he said, Henrietta.

HENRIETTA: (*Breathlessly.*) Of course—one can so seldom anticipate. But tell me—your dream, Stephen? It means——?

STEVE: It means—I was considerably surprised by what it means.

HENRIETTA: *Don't* be so exasperating!

STEVE: It means—you really want to know, Henrietta?

HENRIETTA: Stephen, you'll drive me mad!

STEVE: He said—of course he may be wrong in what he said.

HENRIETTA: He *isn't* wrong. *Tell* me!

STEVE: He said my dreams of the walls receding and

leaving me alone in a forest indicates a suppressed desire——

HENRIETTA: Yes—yes!

STEVE: To be freed from——

HENRIETTA: Yes—freed from——?

STEVE: Marriage.

HENRIETTA: (*Crumples. Stares.*) Marriage!

STEVE: He—he may be mistaken, you know.

HENRIETTA: *May* be mistaken!

STEVE: I—well, of course, I hadn't taken any stock in it myself. It was only your great confidence——

HENRIETTA: Stephen, are you telling me that Dr. Russell—Dr. A. E. Russell—told you this? (*Steve nods.*) Told you you have a suppressed desire to separate from me?

STEVE: That's what he said.

HENRIETTA: Did he know who you were?

STEVE: Yes.

HENRIETTA: That you were married to me?

STEVE: Yes, he knew that.

HENRIETTA: And he told you to leave me?

STEVE: It seems he must be wrong, Henrietta.

HENRIETTA: (*Rising.*) And I've sent him more patients——! (*Catches herself and resumes coldly.*) What reason did he give for this analysis?

STEVE: He says the confining walls are a symbol of my feeling about marriage and that their fading away is a wish-fulfillment.

HENRIETTA: (*Gulping.*) Well, is it? Do you want our marriage to end?

STEVE: Well, it was a great surprise to me that I did, Henrietta. You see I hadn't known what was in my unconscious mind.

HENRIETTA: (*Flaming.*) What did you tell Dr. Russell about me to make him think you weren't happy?

STEVE: I never told him a thing, Henrietta. He got it all from his confounded clever inferences. I—I tried to refute them, but he said that was only part of my self-protective lying.

HENRIETTA: And that's why you were so—happy—when you came in just now!

STEVE: Why, Henrietta, how can you say such a thing? I was *sad*. Didn't I speak sadly of—of the view? Didn't I ask how long we had been married?

HENRIETTA: (*Rising.*) Stephen Brewster, have you no sense of the seriousness of this? Dr. Russell doesn't know what our marriage has been. You do. You should have laughed him down! Confined—in life with me? Did you tell him that I believe in freedom?

STEVE: I very emphatically told him that his results were a great surprise to me.

HENRIETTA: But you accepted them.

STEVE: Oh, not at all. I merely couldn't refute his arguments. I'm not a psychologist. I came home to talk it over with you. You being a disciple of psychoanalysis——

HENRIETTA: If you are going, I wish you would go tonight!

STEVE: Oh, my dear! I—surely I couldn't do that! Think of my feelings. And my laundry hasn't come home.

HENRIETTA: I ask you to go tonight. Some women would falter at this, Steve, but I am not such a woman. I leave you free. I do not repudiate psychoanalysis, I say again that it has done great things. It has also made mistakes, of course. But since you accept this analysis— (*She sits down and pretends to begin work.*) I have to finish this paper. I wish you would leave me.

STEVE: (*Scratches his head, goes to the inner door.*) I'm sorry, Henrietta, about my unconscious mind.

(*Exit. Henrietta's face betrays her outraged state of mind—disconcerted, resentful, trying to pull herself together. She attains an air of bravely bearing an outrageous thing. Mabel enters in great excitement.*)

MABEL: (*Breathless.*) Henrietta, I'm so glad you're here. And alone? (*Looks toward the inner door.*) Are you alone, Henrietta?

HENRIETTA: (*With reproving dignity.*) Very much so.

MABEL: (*Rushing to her.*) Henrietta, he's found it!

HENRIETTA: (*Aloof.*) Who has found what?

MABEL: Who has found what? Dr. Russell has found my suppressed desire.

HENRIETTA: That is interesting.

MABEL: He finished with me today—he got hold of my complex—in the most amazing way! But, oh, Henrietta—it is so terrible!

HENRIETTA: Do calm yourself, Mabel. Surely there's no occasion for all this agitation.

MABEL: But there is! And when you think of the lives that are affected—the readjustments that must be made in order to bring the suppressed hell out of me and save me from the insane asylum——!

HENRIETTA: The insane asylum!

MABEL: You said that's where these complexes brought people?

HENRIETTA: What did the doctor tell you, Mabel?

MABEL: Oh, I don't know how I can tell you—it is so awful—so unbelievable.

HENRIETTA: I rather have my hand in at hearing the unbelievable.

MABEL: Henrietta, who would ever have thought it? How can it be true? But the doctor is perfectly certain that I have a suppressed desire for—(*Looks at Henrietta unable to go on.*)

HENRIETTA: Oh, go on, Mabel. I'm not unprepared for what you have to say.

MABEL: Not unprepared? You mean you have suspected it?

HENRIETTA: From the first. It's been my theory all along.

MABEL: But, Henrietta, I didn't know myself that I had this secret desire for Stephen.

HENRIETTA: (*Jumps up.*) Stephen!

MABEL: My brother-in-law! My own sister's husband!

HENRIETTA: *You* have a suppressed desire for *Stephen!*

MABEL: Oh, Henrietta, aren't these unconscious selves terrible? They seem so unlike us!

HENRIETTA: What insane thing are you driving at?

MABEL: (*Blubbering.*) Henrietta, don't you use that word to me. I don't *want* to go to the insane asylum.

HENRIETTA: What did Dr. Russell say?

MABEL: Well, you see—oh, it's the strangest thing! But you know the voice in my dream that called "Step, Hen!" Dr. Russell found out today that when I was a little girl I had a story-book in words of one syllable and I read the name Stephen wrong. I used to read it S-t-e-p, step, h-e-n, hen. (*Dramatically.*) Step Hen is Stephen. (*Enter Stephen, his head bent over a time-table.*) Stephen is Step Hen!

STEVE: I? Step Hen!

MABEL: (*Triumphantly.*) S-t-e-p, step, H-e-n, hen, Stephen!

HENRIETTA: (*Exploding.*) Well, what if Stephen is Step Hen? (*Scornfully.*) Step Hen! Step Hen!! For that ridiculous coincidence——

MABEL: Coincidence! But it's childish to look at the mere elements of a dream. You have to look into it—you have to see what it means!

HENRIETTA: On account of that trivial, meaningless play on syllables—on that flimsy basis—you are ready— (*Wails*) O-h!

STEVE: What on earth's the matter? What has happened? Suppose I *am* Step Hen? What about it? What does it mean?

MABEL: (*Crying.*) It means—that I—have a suppressed desire for *you!*

STEVE: For me! The deuce you have? (*Feebly.*) What—er—makes you think so?

MABLE: Dr. Russell has worked it out scientifically.

HENRIETTA: Yes. Through the amazing discovery that Step Hen equals Stephen!

MABEL: (*Tearfully.*) Oh, that isn't all—that isn't near all. Henrietta won't give me a chance to tell it. She'd rather I'd go to the insane asylum than be unconventional.

HENRIETTA: We'll all go there if you can't control yourself. We are still waiting for some rational report.

MABEL: (*Drying her eyes.*) Oh, there's such a lot about names. (*With some pride.*) I don't see how I ever did it. It all works in together. I dreamed I was a hen because that's the first syllable of *Hen*-rietta's name, and when I dreamed I was a hen, I was putting myself in Henrietta's place.

HENRIETTA: With Stephen?

MABEL: With Stephen.

HENRIETTA: (*Outraged.*) Oh! (*Turns in rage upon Stephen, who is fanning himself with the time-table.*) What are you doing with that time-table?

STEVE: Why—I thought—you were so keen to have me go tonight—I thought I'd just take a run up to Canada, and join Billy—a little shooting—but——

MABEL: But there's more about the names.

HENRIETTA: Mabel, have you thought of Bob—dear old Bob—your good, kind husband?

MABEL: Oh, Henrietta, "my good, kind husband!"

HENRIETTA: Think of him, Mabel, out there alone in Chicago, working his head off, fixing people's teeth—for *you!*

MABEL: Yes, but think of the living Libido—in conflict with petrified moral codes! And think of the perfectly wonderful way the names all prove it. Dr. Russell said he's never seen anything more convincing. Just look at Stephen's last name—Brewster. I dream I'm a hen, and the name Brewster—you have to say its first letter by itself—and then the hen, that's me, she says to him: "Stephen, Be Rooster!"

Henrietta and Stephen both collapse on chair and divan.

MABEL: I think it's perfectly wonderful! Why, if it wasn't for psychoanalysis you'd never find out how wonderful your own mind is!

STEVE: (*Begins to chuckle.*) Be Rooster, Stephen, Be Rooster!

HENRIETTA: You think it's funny, do you?

STEVE: Well, what's to be done about it? Does Mabel have to go away with me?

HENRIETTA: Do you want Mabel to go away with you?

STEVE: Well, but Mabel herself—her complex—her suppressed desire——!

HENRIETTA: Mabel, are you going to insist on going away with Stephen?

MABEL: I'd rather go with Stephen than go to the insane asylum!

HENRIETTA: For Heaven's sake, Mabel, drop that insane asylum! If you *did* have a suppressed desire for Stephen hidden away in you—God knows it isn't hidden *now.* Dr. Russell has brought it into your consciousness —with a vengeance. That's all that's necessary to break up a complex. Psychoanalysis doesn't say you have to *gratify* every suppressed desire.

STEVE: (*Softly.*) Unless it's for Lyman Eggleston.

HENRIETTA: (*Turning on him.*) Well, if it comes to that, Stephen Brewster, I'd like to know why that interpretation of mine isn't as good as this one? Step, Hen!

STEVE: But Be Rooster! (*He pauses, chuckling to himself.*) Step-Hen B-rooster. And *H*enrietta. Pshaw, my dear, Doc Russell's got you beat a mile! (*He turns away and chuckles.*) Be rooster!

MABEL: What has Lyman Eggleston got to do with it?

STEVE: According to Henrietta, you, the hen, have a suppressed desire for *Egg*leston, the egg.

MABEL: Henrietta, I think that's indecent of you! He is bald as an egg and little and fat—the idea of you thinking such a thing of me!

HENRIETTA: Well, Bob isn't little and bald and fat! Why don't you stick to your own husband? (*Turns on Stephen.*) What if Dr. Russell's interpretation has got mine "beat a mile"? (*Resentful look at him.*) It would only mean that Mabel doesn't want Eggleston and does want you. Does that mean she has to have you?

MABEL: But you said Mabel Snow——

HENRIETTA: *Mary* Snow! You're not as much like her as you think—substituting your name for hers! The cases are entirely different. Oh, I wouldn't have believed this of you, Mabel. I brought you here for a pleasant visit—thought you needed brightening up—wanted to be nice to you—and now you—my husband—you insist— (*Begins to cry. Makes a movement which brushes to the floor some sheets from the psychoanalytical table.*)

STEVE: (*With solicitude.*) Careful, dear. Your paper on psychoanalysis! (*Gathers up sheets and offers them to her.*)

HENRIETTA: (*Crying.*) I don't want my paper on psychoanalysis! I'm sick of psychoanalysis!

STEVE: (*Eagerly.*) Do you mean that, Henrietta?

HENRIETTA: Why shouldn't I mean it? Look at all I've done for psychoanalysis—and—what has psychoanalysis done for me?

STEVE: Do you mean, Henrietta, that you're going to stop talking psychoanalysis?

HENRIETTA: Why shouldn't I stop talking it? Haven't I seen what it does to people? Mabel has gone crazy about psychoanalysis! (*At the word "crazy" Mabel sinks with a moan into the armchair and buries her face in her hands.*)

STEVE: (*Solemnly.*) Do you swear never to wake me up in the night to find out what I'm dreaming?

HENRIETTA: Dream what you please—I don't care what you're dreaming.

STEVE: Will you clear off my work-table so the Journal of Morbid Psychology doesn't stare me in the face when I'm trying to plan a house?

HENRIETTA: (*Pushing a stack of periodicals off the table.*) I'll *burn* the Journal of Morbid Psychology!

STEVE: My dear Henrietta, if you're going to separate from psychoanalysis, there's no reason why I should separate from you. (*They embrace ardently. Mabel lifts her head and looks at them woefully.*)

MABEL: (*Jumping up and going toward them.*) But what about me? What am I to do with my suppressed desire?

STEVE: (*With one arm still around Henrietta, gives Mabel a brotherly hug.*) Mabel, you just keep right on suppressing it.

CURTAIN.

www.ingramcontent.com/pod-product-compliance
Lightning Source LLC
Chambersburg PA
CBHW051706040426
42446CB00009B/1332